LEADERSHIP —— OVER —— LONELINESS

*How Unleashing the Leader Within
Transformed My Life*

Ethan Spelman

No part of this publication may be reproduced, stored in a retrieval system, or transmitted in any form or by any means — electronic, photocopying, recording, or otherwise — without prior written permission, except in the case of brief excerpts in critical reviews and articles. For permission requests, contact the author at www.ethanspelman.com.

All rights reserved.

Copyright © 2024 Ethan Spelman

Cover photo of New York's Canandaigua Lake taken by the author.

Writing and editing support provided by
Martial Bednar Communications, LLC.

ISBN: 9798321238523 (Paperback)
ISBN: 9798321238813 (Hardcover)

The author disclaims responsibility for adverse effects or consequences from the misapplication or injudicious use of the information contained in this book. Mention of resources and associations does not imply an endorsement.

*Dedicated to my family, friends, and the true leaders
who have inspired me on my journey.*

*Your support of this new chapter in my life
has made all the difference.*

Table of Contents

Preface 1

Part I: A Life of Loneliness 5
Chapter 1 *Answering the Call*..............................7
Chapter 2 *Becoming Self-Aware*........................13
Chapter 3 *Baggage* 17
Chapter 4 *Young and Lonely* 19
Chapter 5 *Mom and Dad* 25
Chapter 6 *Run and Hide* 31
Chapter 7 *Finding Myself*...................................37
Chapter 8 *Then and Now* 43

Part II: Lessons in Leadership 49
Chapter 9   *Don't Stop Evolving* 51
Chapter 10 *Accept Change* 57
Chapter 11 *Lean In and Pour In*..........................63
Chapter 12 *Fear Not!* 69
Chapter 13 *Be Self-Aware, Not Self-Absorbed* 75
Chapter 14 *Learn from Mistakes and Failure* 79
Chapter 15 *Listen…and Gain Perspective* 85
Chapter 16 *Remove the Masks: Forgive, Accept, and Be Vulnerable*................91

Chapter 17 *Be Courageous* 97
Chapter 18 *Mindset Matters!* 103

Unleashed: *The Leader and the Man Within* 109

Preface

"*Are you courageous enough to tell your own story?*"

I was asked this rhetorical question when I took part in a candid video interview about courage and leadership more than three years ago. And for most of my life, the question was a very easy one to answer – always with a resounding "NO."

That's because I've always been fearful. Fearful of being lonely. Of doing something wrong. Of not being good enough. Of failure. Of what others might think.

And certainly of my past.

But in recent years, something happened along my life's journey: Yes, I've grown a bit older and wiser, both personally and professionally. But I've also been working hard to become more courageous and not allow fear to overwhelm my courage, as it has for most of my life. The shift occurred when I immersed myself in the power of leadership done right.

So this is my story – and I'm sharing it because I believe it is one that can bring hope, courage, inspiration, and maybe even conviction to others.

I believe that as we age, we move from being immersed in life to wondering what our purpose is in this same life. To look back isn't always a bad thing (as some may think), but remaining in the past definitely holds us back and stunts our growth.

John Maxwell, the world renowned leadership expert who has inspired me tremendously, once said, "Life is 10 percent of what happens to us and 90 percent of how we respond to it." But for years, I lived in the reverse: I allowed my fears and shame to be my 90 percent. It is only until I began learning the importance of self-awareness in my relationships with others that I began to change the narrative of my own life.

I hope that by typing these words, sharing my personal story, and navigating through my past that I will begin to gain clarity on what lies ahead.

I am writing this for myself – as pouring myself into leadership has allowed me to reframe my story and has helped me overcome the many obstacles of my past. I also write for those who are on their own journey of discovery through transformation. But to just share my personal story isn't enough. It is more than that: It is how the lessons of leadership have helped me arrive at this place of self-discovery and view my own evolution as a way to help inspire others.

My story, sadly, begins in a place of loneliness, silence, darkness, and confusion. I used to try to control the outcome of every scenario. But I have learned that you can't grow and control. To control means there is an end. My journey is far from over – so I have chosen to grow and help others grow with me. And while my story started a long time ago, my transformation continues today.

PART I

A Life of Loneliness

CHAPTER 1

Answering the Call

Throughout my 25-year career, I have held several leadership positions in financial services. I've experienced both personal and professional success, but not without numerous mistakes. So in 2017, I took a break from leadership and went into personal sales production. I was in a place that made me question my path and abilities.

Ironically, when I stepped away from leading others and focused more on leading myself, I was reminded by others how I helped them – even though leading people wasn't in my job description. But as I reflect on it, my prior experience in leadership was in title only and superficial. Yet in its absence, I realized that I had left leadership only to discover that I wasn't fulfilled without it. Back then, what I didn't understand was the need to dig deeper to get better.

I always knew that the real leader in me was buried deep inside. That explains why throughout my early career,

I had a leather volleyball folder from the 1996 Summer Olympics in which I stored leadership notes, memories, feelings, and inspiration that I had accumulated over the years. I always told myself that I would share these when I wrote my story.

Little did I think back then that it would ever actually happen.

Back in 2017, I was introduced to John Maxwell's leadership program and philosophy, which definitely spoke to me. I had a preliminary conversation with their team and learned what was involved both financially and in the time it would take to become a certified coach and trainer. I liked the story very much, but feared the expense, the commitment, and whether or not I could really do it. So I ignored the calls and remained stuck where I was – kidding myself that I was content.

Looking back, I can honestly say that I didn't even begin to understand what it meant to invest in myself. I was resting on how others saw me as a leader and my day-to-day proverbial motions to succeed. But was I succeeding? By the time I made the initial call to John Maxwell, I had three different roles in three years: different organizations, more responsibility. But I was lost in the chase – seeking fulfillment and searching for answers. In that search, I was subconsciously choosing to ignore the voice inside of me, which was craving more – not from others, but for myself.

Fast forward two years, to summer 2019. It was then when I began to learn the value of self-worth through one of the most challenging and lonely times in my life.

My father-in-law had played a role of quiet strength in our family since I came into it 20 years earlier. Bob loved to talk with and learn about people. We used to joke (and at times cringe!) about some of the questions he asked. But he was unapologetic in his questioning, as it was built into his inquisitive nature. He had a way to make you feel important in the moment. He was a leader by trade – and as I think back, a leader before his time. Today much is made about vulnerability and getting to know the person or people you lead. Bob did just that. He was a divisional supervisor in retail. It wasn't glamorous. He traveled and worked long hours, but he did it his way: leading through learning people. It wasn't about punching a clock, it was about understanding, leveraging, and growing through others. Bob was able to leverage his questions to strengthen relationships and gain respect. I don't believe I am overstating to say his leadership style was well ahead of his time and one that would be welcomed today. He had a way of respecting everyone. And in what may seem lost today, Bob had an ability to seek to understand as opposed to being divisive in argument and only acknowledging his perspective.

Those traits stayed with him until the day before his death from a four-year battle with cancer on August 8, 2019.

The day before he died, he gathered his family together and spent time individually with each one of us. Talking. Asking. Listening. He then brought everyone together and although in pain wanted to make sure we all had the opportunity to share, listen, and know of his deep love and respect for his family. He wanted to die as he lived – and ensure we knew it, too. He had no regrets.

I believe to this day he knew he gave us all a parting gift. What an incredible display of love and leadership when it mattered most.

The next morning, Bob passed away. When the call came, that indelible moment became completely debilitating.

I was asked – and humbled – by my wife's family to write and deliver the eulogy to capture and share Bob's magnificent life through my words, using my experience and the memories of others. I was honored. And the experience created a new inner confidence in me. Although feeling sad and empty at times, I was able to fill the room with incredible memories and heartfelt emotion. I witnessed everyone in that room sensing, feeling, and celebrating my father-in-law through me. That brought me immense peace and I felt Bob and his leadership speaking inside me. An inner drive was ignited in me to continue this journey that I didn't even know had begun that day.

The day after the funeral, it was back to reality. I boarded a plane to fly from Rochester, New York, to San Diego for a work conference. Emotionally drained from the prior week, I remember being on the plane feeling so alone. I began to think and reflect, grateful for the time and space to do just that. I reflected on my words spoken at Bob's funeral, my recollection of a man I truly admired, and his ability to lead relationships through conversation, questioning, and listening. I reflected intensely on our personal conversation the day before he died and took comfort and inspiration in how he saw me today and what he saw for me in the future.

It was in that moment of loneliness and darkness when it hit me: I finally realized that I was being chosen and called to lead at a deeper level. I was being challenged to learn more about myself more broadly...to forgive myself...to invest in myself...to help myself lead others.

I didn't know what it all meant, or what was ahead, but leadership was calling me through that moment of deep loneliness and even deeper awareness of love. So after I landed, I picked up my phone, found my contacts at John Maxwell from two years prior, scheduled a new call, and said YES. Let's start!

I made my first intentional decision of growth and leadership for myself and others. And it felt great.

In a time of tremendous loneliness and uncertainty in my life, I learned and consciously chose inner strength through self-reflection, self-investment, and leading others with discipline and intention. In that moment of intense loneliness,

I chose the road less traveled – one that has forced me to learn uncomfortable truths, to be open to learn from others, and most importantly to leverage the memory and continued spirit of my father-in-law and his words to remind me that I will be OK.

In doing so, I began facing and understanding my fears and becoming more self-aware of my actions so I can help others and lead them through their own journey. Through it all, life has shown itself in mysterious ways. Four months after my commitment to John Maxwell and a new journey, leadership came calling. I was called to where I am today, leading others in their work and, in some instances, their life. I answered that call with arms – and heart – wide open.

And I continue to learn along the journey.

CHAPTER 2

Becoming Self-Aware

Looking inside ourselves can be one of the most challenging things we ever do. To stay at the surface, to focus on the day to day, and to project what we feel others want (or need) to see can easily be the norm in anyone's journey.

But how is that being aware?

When we let life control us, we lose focus on the one person who makes the most difference in our lives: OURSELVES.

My transformation began later in life. When I began to wonder why I am who I am, I was left to sort through the stacks of masks that were inside. I never felt like I was being fake, but I was taught from a very early age to be what and who others expected me to be – to meet their expectations and not to step out of the lane intended for me.

As I "matured" (if you call it that!) into my teenage years, I did what teenagers do: challenged and ultimately rejected the perceived norms. Instead of using that time to understand and learn, I ran the other way – literally (with more on that to come). I pushed away and rode through my teen years in cruise control. I found myself in many compromising situations and taught myself to morph to the expectation of the moment. To live in the lane that was created by choices I was making. It was never about me and what I wanted; it was always about pleasing others around me. And I was learning through their satisfaction.

Looking inside myself and reliving the mistakes, the loss, and the loneliness scares me even today. As leaders we often strive to help others see and define their self-worth. But where was mine? I have learned through my ongoing journey of awareness that my self-worth initially came from my past.

I also have learned that my journey of self-introspection and awareness is not finite. It is a commitment and a choice. For years, I chose to ignore what was inside me. I have hidden behind choices that were reckless, self-deprecating, and isolating. I have denied my past and ignored those in it to pretend it didn't exist. I always was left to feel I didn't match up. It led to a life of emptiness and feeling unfulfilled at times. The choices I have made to fill the voids blinded me to my values and what was important to me. I chose the moment as opposed to myself. My choices hurt many – most importantly, myself. As I am learning self-awareness, I am learning that choices to fill the void instead of choices to fuel the person are a lousy way to live.

We always hear that to love others, we must first love ourselves. To love as we should requires trust and forgiveness. It is not wise for us to keep looking back; we should be taking steps forward, knowing we are all a work in progress and that we are all human. Humans make mistakes! It is how we learn from those mistakes and the choices we make going forward that help us on our journey.

That said, my journey of self-awareness has forced me into some uncomfortable and at times compromising internal work. To look back and forgive myself for choices made, failures along the way, paths ventured, and trusting that I can be myself with others have been difficult both internally and externally. It has challenged me as a friend, a husband, a sibling, a son, and a father.

The journey to become self-aware takes true discipline. It forces me to remind myself that I can't help or lead others along their journey without being able to lead myself in the way I see others needing to be led: in honesty and faith.

Self-awareness is the "superpower" I am hoping to achieve in my journey of leadership and life. But there is plenty of "kryptonite" out there that can destroy – self-doubt, past hurt, lack of trust to love myself, and so much more. I know I am not alone in fighting these demons every day, but each day I gain new perspective and strength along the journey.

I am happy to say that the energy I once spent on denial and self-doubt I now pour into others through leadership, leading with purpose, and helping others navigate the challenging paths they encounter along their own journey of life. That's what great leaders do – and why I'm working so hard to be one.

CHAPTER 3

Baggage

I believe it was Bill Clinton who once said, "Sometimes we bring our baggage to life." I find this simple statement to be a true representation of my past, my journey, and my life experiences.

From my very beginning, it seems like there was baggage. Lots of it. Baggage and expectations of life surrounded me, and I never learned the tools or ways needed to understand and utilize the challenges to avoid more hurt – or bring greater awareness into my life.

To be honest, it started even before I was born. The story goes that my mom (who at one time lived as a nun) was not sure my dad was "the right person" before they got married. It was only after he committed to converting to Catholicism (he was not a religious person) that she decided to proceed with their marriage. Now, you could argue to just trust your gut – but if I can be selfish for a moment, I was born and am alive because of this choice.

My birth wasn't easy from what I've been told. I was born with a hole in my heart and it was severe enough that a priest was brought in to baptize me in the hospital. They even considered Last Rites for me. If that wasn't bad enough, I was named Ethan Howard Spelman (Howard was my dad's middle name). But by the time I was brought home from the hospital, my Mom had changed my name to Ethan Taylor Spelman to reflect her family name.

Now, some may say that it's just a name – get over it. But to me, this symbolizes the beginning of not understanding who I was. It laid the groundwork for learning life through my mom's eyes and not getting a chance to learn and live through who I was or could become.

So the baggage began building at my birth, and for years continued to weigh on and tear away at my inner self. And although the physical hole in my heart may have healed itself in time, a much bigger hole of emptiness and loneliness was growing inside of me.

CHAPTER 4

Young and Lonely

It's 1976: America turned 200. I turned four.

It's hard to believe I can recall this, but I distinctly remember being in my dining room, feeling alone. It's the first time I was introduced to the "empty feeling" – as I referred to it growing up, and still do today. I have learned to live with that feeling throughout my life, and believe that it is my awareness of that feeling that ignites my internal fight to grow and evolve.

Looking back on that day, I have no idea where my mom and dad were. All I remember is standing there and being overwhelmed by THAT feeling.

That painful, empty, alone feeling was one I experienced a lot growing up. I remember sharing it with my mom but not being able to define it. Just writing about it now, I can still feel the emptiness and not explain where it comes from or why. But it began that day in 1976 in my dining room. That I absolutely remember.

Ironically, that was the same year my sister was born and I was no longer the only child. Was there a correlation there? Maybe. I remember being at the hospital when she was born. Not being a part of much, just being present. Sadly, I have no more memories from that year or the transitional growth of our family. (At the same time, I struggle to remember things that happened yesterday!) Reaching back into the memory banks over the years may simply be asking too much.

However, that one memory was profound enough to stick with me throughout my life. It has never left my side or my heart. Although I had no idea at the time, I have always felt that day's meaning was in and of itself a defining moment of what I would experience over the next several years.

When I was six years old, my parents made a choice – one that to this day, I will never understand. But one that only seemed to steamroll the impact of my feeling alone and my constant struggle to feel accepted. The choice was to expand our family through adoption. Not just with any child, but one with disabilities and a very challenging background. There wasn't even a trial run; there was a meeting at the zoo to meet the boy who was the same age as me and would now become my brother.

To me, this was like a bomb had been dropped without a thought of the potential impact on the entire family. The family dynamic that may have been there prior to this decision was now blown to pieces – but to the outside world, it appeared like all was great: we were this bold, amazing, and trailblazing family.

I truly believe that this new focus filled my mother's intense desire to be needed and to potentially fill a space of loneliness she had in her own life.

The immediate impact? My dad's parents disowned the family because my new brother was African-American. I didn't know that until later in life; I just knew then that they stopped coming around – and that I ultimately lost a piece of my family connection that I would never know. Of course, that choice also impacted my dad and his relationship with his parents, which I am sure had a dramatic impact on him as well.

The second and more profound effect: the collision of the disparate backgrounds that were introduced and merged, totally haphazardly. The needs and focus of my family shifted almost immediately to ensure my new brother's acceptance into our family. Looking back now, I can see how this just took the emptiness I was already feeling and allowed it to grow and fester inside me and with me. I remember asking about and sharing my empty feeling with my mom.

She never took it seriously.

That's because, as if one bomb wasn't enough, my parents dropped another one: They decided to adopt again less than two years later.

Were we not enough??!

This time it was a one-and-a-half year old bi-racial girl. She came from a background of abuse, and had disabilities likely caused by the abuse she endured.

One year later, we received a call that a baby was born to a mother who was addicted to drugs.

She became my third sister, after being released from the hospital.

It didn't take long before there were stories and photos of my family in the newspaper. From the outside, we were viewed as this "super family." Inside the walls and in my world, however, it was anything but super. My already wobbly foundation was shaken to its core. It was never developed and was not being supported. Cracks were everywhere. The hole in my physical heart may have long healed, but by now there was no way to heal my deeply broken heart. That feeling of emptiness grew even bigger, as did my need to seek acceptance from the outside.

By the time I was 10, I had lived in three different towns, five different homes, and enrolled in six different schools. The bombings of my early life left shrapnel everywhere. Change and "running" seemed like the only escape

– not just for me, but for my mom, my dad, and their demons as well.

CHAPTER 5

Mom and Dad

There have been numerous studies done on the role of parents – both individually and collectively – in the growth and emotional well-being of children. Being a parent comes with sacrifice. Parents often sacrifice parts of their life to ensure their children get what they need or often want.

And as we all know, there is no job description or how-to manual on how to do this most important job in the world.

Sadly, my mom was the opposite of most mothers. I believe she sacrificed her children's needs for her own, and made decisions that made her feel better at the expense of the stability of the intertwined family she built – but did not strive to grow. From my perspective, her focus and drive seemed to be on building and moving: Build more and move, until she was left standing there with nothing but rubble because the foundation was never stable.

I often wonder: Did my loneliness stem from her inability to fill her own needs? Did she even know what her needs were? Did she ever realize that she was incapable of being a support to me because she didn't know who she was herself?

I think back to the times when I needed her. I remember being a young boy…coming into the room because of a bad dream, wanting to crawl into bed with my parents. I was told to sleep in the dog's bed. And you know what? I did. There was a fan blowing and no blanket. I huddled into this bed made for a dog for the rest of the night, waiting for daylight.

The next morning, my parents saw me and laughed it off.

I also remember developing a fear of dying and lived with this fear from an early age. It was overwhelming. I was in fourth grade – which was the fifth school I had been enrolled in by then. (Yes: five schools by fourth grade.) I had a young gym teacher who died suddenly of an aneurysm. This was my first experience with death, and I remember being so confused. I began to fear death, and believed I too would be dead at an early age. Then, in 1985, my Uncle John died suddenly. He was in his late thirties as I remember. It happened when he was at work.

Our relationship was special. Uncle John always said I was the son he never had. Our families were close and he was my sister's godfather. He took me to my first-ever

Buffalo Bills training camp, which is the reason I am the fan I am today. I remember getting the news and crying so hard. But I cried alone. We never talked about it as a family. We never went through the funeral process, so I never got to deal with it or even say goodbye. This created yet another void in my life, and I became certain I would die at age 36.

I look back now and wonder why as a family we weren't able to learn at that moment. My intense loneliness only expanded and began to morph into a fear of dying. Maybe it was just a part of it, or the result of the empty feeling I lived with. I truly wanted to talk to my mom about my feelings, but couldn't. But I tried. I often talked about this empty feeling I felt and how I was living with this fear of loneliness and death. But sadly, my mom never tried to understand, nor did she really seem to care. The opportunity was there to share, to love, to teach, to discuss death. But like other times when death happened around us, it was not dealt with or discussed. As I have now come to learn, death is our first experience of the reality of life. We are all going to die. But death allows us to learn and appreciate the blessings of life. Growing up, those opportunities were lost on me and only amplified the loneliness I was living.

But our family was all about its appearance and ensuring that from the outside, everything looked good. All at the expense of what was breaking inside. In a way, it's similar to how someone might view my home today: If you walk in, everything looks neat and organized. Just don't open the cupboards or closets!

This metaphor resonates in my heart. The struggle to continue my journey of transformation is still real.

As I share all of this about my mother, I realize I have not said a whole lot about my father. Some may read this and wonder if I give him a pass in the struggles I had as a child. I can accept that, and at times I think I did.

The bottom line was that until I was 11, my dad was part of my life. After that – because of the inevitable divorce that was to come (and more that I will share) – my dad's presence was very limited at the exact same time I needed it the most: as an adolescent. I don't know who to blame for that, but suffice it to say that his role as a father was not a leading one in my early years.

I remember always wanting more from him. There are pictures of me on his shoulders, but I don't remember a hug. There were moments when he took me on early morning paper routes with him, but "I love you" was never spoken. I remember being on a canoe with my dad, but he never taught me how to fish. I heard how he was a swimmer growing up, but this athlete never threw a ball to me. I remember being in Little League but never seeing him (or my mom) in the stands – even though he was the president of the league. Instead, our time together was often about getting things done on his schedule – like shopping on Saturdays, or pulling pond grass when it needed to be done.

Not having wonderful memories with my own dad makes me sad and still hurts at times. But my father probably felt the same way as a child. He was the son of an alcoholic, and became one himself. Fortunately, he is now recovered – but that doesn't change the fact that I too am the son of an alcoholic. So that feeling of detachment may just come with the territory. He didn't have a role model of his own, but I am not sure he tried to learn or be different.

All of this was clearly a factor in my loneliness and empty feeling that I've struggled with throughout my life. I always wondered if I mattered to him, if I was accepted, or if I was doing enough to make him proud. His respect and love always seemed based on whether or not his children met his expectations of the situation or the time we spent together. This was another theme that was intertwined into my life then… and for years to come.

So how did all of this affect my fight and desire to become a better person? As a father myself, I could have chosen the path my dad did with his kids. Instead, I chose to become the best dad I could be. I remind myself of the loneliness and disconnected relationship we had (and still have) as father and son. I use that loneliness and my imperfections to remind me to be present for my kids. I do all I can to show love and let them know how proud I am of them as people – not just when they succeed, but when they struggle as well.

I fail at times. But that's OK. I own it, and they see it.

And they've known since they were just little kids how very much they are loved by their parents.

CHAPTER 6

Run and Hide

Fast-forward to 1983. MTV turns two, and is going strong. I turn 11, and am hanging on by a thread.

Once again, we are being introduced to another new member of the family. This time it was a foster child with the option to adopt. The boy was four years older than me and came from a juvenile home. He had been burned by his mother at two years old and half his body had scars from head to toe. His sad story and years of pain were now being forced into our story.

The talk was of an eventual adoption, until the family meeting in August 1983.

The "meeting" was to share the news that my dad was leaving the family, and planning to divorce my mom. The weak foundation I had long been standing on suddenly caved in. I remember being sad, numb, and confused. The dysfunctional life we were already living was never going to be the same.

There were no further discussions.

My dad walked out, came back for his clothes, and left again. There was no checking to see if I was OK, helping me understand, or reinforcing any love.

The first shoe to drop involved sending my new foster brother back to his juvenile home. Then we moved to another new town, another new school, and into a new home with my grandparents (my mom's parents, of course). My search for acceptance took another backseat to my mom's anger and sadness and her own battles internally.

My mom said that my dad left because of us kids – and that he no longer wanted us. We eventually had recurring supervised visits with my dad for seven hours every other week. My mom would leave the house, but my grandparents stayed. After multiple missed visits and broken visitation promises, he seemed to get his own life in sync. It became convenient for him to visit and the supervision requirement was lifted.

Mom made the immediate rule that we could no longer call my dad "Dad" inside our house; he was to be referred to by his first and last name only. If there was any written or phone communication with him, it was monitored and in some cases rewritten by my mom to fit her narrative, not our thoughts or feelings. Again, this reinforced that underlying inability to understand our feelings and created more of that gap between self and the need for validation and understanding.

The loneliness kept growing.

By the time I was 12, I had gone from being alone and empty to having the narrative of my life changed. I had no real understanding of the emotions I felt, but was living – no, make that existing – through the feelings and thoughts of the totally broken person that my Mother embodied. I was unable to share my perspective and be heard for what I needed or felt, and was in no uncertain terms told to shut up and fall in line.

So I found myself searching for acceptance from anyone. I went to church daily with my grandmother at a monastery – sometimes as early as 5:30 a.m. It felt disconnected from the world in which I lived, and I felt accepted and even noticed for who I was. I was befriended by a good and decent priest and even was curious about possibly joining the monks because the monastery seemed like a safe and isolated place to be. Of course, I was too young.

That man wanted to spend time with me. He would leave the monastery to bike to my house to visit and talk baseball. I found out later he got reprimanded for leaving the premises multiple times, but I am guessing (hopefully maybe) that he sensed the terrible void I felt inside and the brokenness I was living in. I will always hold a place in my heart for this good man and all I believe he TRIED to do in his limited capacity to help save a boy who was searching for inclusion and wanted to be seen and understood.

After frequenting the monastery numerous times, my mom entrusted me to adults who spent time there. Before long, she was quick to send her 12-year-old son out for day trips, movies, or dinners with single, adult men. For a boy starving for attention from his father, these men became my "friends" until they weren't. This only stunted my ability to make friends my own age.

What could possibly go wrong with that?

This is extremely difficult to share, but by the time I became a teenager, I was involved in sexual abuse and illicit behavior inside my own home. Some would say I was a victim. I understand that, but at that age and where I was in my emotional development, I didn't know enough to know it was wrong until it was eventually uncovered by my mom. Her response? She asked that it stop and to not discuss it moving forward. The silence created yet another layer of loneliness and confusion for me, and there was no looking back.

By the time the abuse and activity were discovered and stopped, it had been a couple of years, had happened throughout my whole household, and I was not the only victim.

Even now as I write this, the guilt, shame, distrust, and anger at myself makes me so uncomfortable and resides deep inside me. I do feel like a victim at times and at other times I feel like an enabler because I wasn't able to stop it and it impacted too many. These feelings have haunted me for years and have been entwined in relationships and friendships I have tried to maintain. Even in the midst of the closest relationships and friendships I have and had, I have been immersed in feelings of great loneliness.

I have only just begun to explore the abuse and its impact on my life. I ask myself: What if my mom was more connected? Would she have noticed and stopped it sooner? When it was uncovered, her response was to stop it – but never speak of it again. That makes me question how much she was truly able to help.

I also think of myself, the oldest of six children. The responsibility placed on me for taking care of my siblings failed when I didn't have the tools or understanding to respond to what was happening with me and others inside my own home. Although I was immersed in the abuse, could I have truly played a role in stopping it before it became the entangled web that it did?

I fought for years to not allow this terrible ordeal to define my life's story, and pretended for a long time that it didn't happen or exist. But what I have come to realize through my personal, internal work is that this tragedy will not define my life – but the trauma and shame have indeed played a super-sized role in my loneliness, my friendship and relationship failures, and the true narrative of the man I am today.

What do I see when I look back at that awful time? It was confusing. It was shameful. I lost the value of my own self-worth. I was left to question my own sexuality and my role in the pain and fear. I had lost any chance to love myself. That had been stolen from me and I needed to find a way to bury it all. Ultimately, I built terrible coping mechanisms: drinking, lying, stealing, and cheating. I couldn't hold a relationship or sustain a friendship.

At 18, after my high school graduation, I officially became a runaway. I threw a party at my house, took a duffel bag of clothes, left a note, and moved in with a friend for a short while. I simply chose not to face or deal with everything and sought acceptance elsewhere. I decided to go to a nearby two-year college and eventually moved in with my dad and his wife.

My mom's response to that move? She threw out everything I had left behind and asked that I not communicate with my brothers and sisters. If I was to ever come to visit, I needed to knock – just as a stranger would.

My existence had been fully erased.

I was left to pick up the pieces based on the choices I made – or, more accurately, were made for me. I continued searching to fill the voids that were expanding, but didn't have the foundation to stabilize them.

CHAPTER 7

Finding Myself

Remember the '90s? I found a comment online that perfectly summed up that wild decade – and accurately defined my wild life at that time: "The 90s was a decade of extremes and contradictions."

I was too.

As an 18-year-old high school graduate and runaway, I was on a path of self-destruction and self-discovery – living a life of extremes and contradictions.

Moving in with my father and his new wife was the best I could do at that time. I was able to do my own thing, and began to build and redefine a foundation for the first time in my life. I realized that living and scraping for food, not working, drinking, and making poor choices – which I had done the summer after leaving my mom's house – was not a sustainable path.

I dove into college headfirst and began pursuing an associate's degree in communications. At that time, I wanted to become a sports broadcaster. Looking back, I liked it for all the wrong reasons: I could be in front of the camera and connect with an audience without truly being connected to anyone.

I was able to land an internship at a local TV station and loved it. I had found my groove! (Or so I thought.) I joined the school newspaper and began to write. I took classes, including public speaking (which I hated and was scared to death of at the time), and spent many hours at the station. Things were really starting to stabilize on the outside and I was headed in a new direction.

But then, everything changed yet again. My dad's wife took a job at the University of Vermont, and they would be moving at the end of my semester.

Seriously?!

So I had two choices: stay local and continue on the path I had begun, but find somewhere else to live and figure it all out on my own. Or, I could move to Vermont with them, find a job, get a year of residency, and get a free education at UVM.

Of course, I chose the "easy way" and moved with them to Burlington, Vermont, the minute my current semester was done. (Doesn't it figure I made the dean's list that semester?!)

The University of Vermont did not offer a communications degree at that time, so I was left to figure it out. By choosing "the easy way," I allowed my broken and disjointed self to be pulled away from one path and be dropped into a world that was unknown and unfamiliar, with no stability and no direction.

Don't get me wrong. I made some good friends and had a lot of fun. But during my first full semester there, all the progress I had made went sideways. Eighteen months later, I failed out of Vermont.

So I reconnected with a former girlfriend and moved back to Upstate New York. I tried to restart my communications degree and internship – and somehow reconnected with my mom.

She was in the process of divorcing her second husband. Looking back now, I realize that she reopened the lines of communication because she "needed" me. She didn't let me move back into her home, but she did let me stay at her guest house on her property and pay rent.

A couple of months later, she announced she was marrying a childhood friend of hers. I remember getting mad and crying. She thought I was concerned for her. In truth, I was mad about the continuing cycle of dysfunction and felt sorry for the childhood friend who I knew was walking into a buzzsaw. Yet again, I was sucked back into a world of expectations and serving her needs. My dad remained in

Vermont; by leaving him and moving back, I made our redefined relationship more divisive.

Nonetheless, I got a job, re-enrolled at school, and somehow completed my associate's degree in 1994. But I had soured on the business of broadcasting and had lost trust in those I counted on to help guide my journey. In addition, my relationship was failing and my path was again getting cloudy. I took out student loans to survive and pay for education that I wasn't even finishing. I started and stopped two more colleges and was at an impasse. I was in and out of relationships. I couldn't find myself – let alone lead myself anywhere.

By 1995, all of the bad habits and the person I had run away from five years earlier were back. I was spiraling into the abyss.

A year later, a friend's wife reached out to me and shared that a local bank was opening branches in a supermarket and was looking for tellers. It definitely wasn't broadcasting, but I realized that ship had sailed. This was a step into something professional! I interviewed and got the job. What's more, I actually liked it.

I wasn't good at it at first, but I could talk to people. I could communicate and relate to others, but didn't have to share much of myself. I got to know customers from behind a counter, and developed my closest friendships during my years at the bank.

After only six months, I was promoted off the teller line. I learned about sales: how to talk with people, the value of listening, and the importance of understanding their needs. I was even recognized in an all-employee meeting for exceeding my sales goals in my first quarter in the position. I was building a foundation in a place I never expected.

Professionally, I was on my way. I was even promoted to branch manager! Two years into my career in banking, I was leading people – at age 26. How could this be? Of course back then, I was simply "managing" my team. But my journey as a leader had begun. I didn't know it then, but as a whole new millennium drew near, I was evolving, growing, and beginning to live my best professional life. I was connecting with people more than I had ever done before, and found myself more in tune to their success than that of my own. Somehow, I was beginning to discover what success tasted like.

Personally, however, I was a hot mess – especially on the relationship front. I did some impulsive and stupid things that I would long regret.

I'll leave it at that.

Just more to add to my long list of failures.

* * *

But miraculously, something happened in the 21st century: I began turning my life around by discovering the leader within.

CHAPTER 8

Then and Now

"*If only I knew then what I know now.*"

I can't tell you how many times I have said this to myself – wanting to go back in time to change an event or experience. So I wonder: Why do we say that? Why do we want to look back to make changes to things we cannot? Why do we struggle to use the past to make changes for the future? We tend to blame the past for the present, which frames our future and limits ourselves to wishing we could change it.

For years, I lived this way. I was unwilling to see the past for what it was, to truly understand its grip and leverage over me and how it shaped decisions I made for my life in the moment.

Through personal work and therapy, I have tried in recent years to get it right: To let go of the past, and not let it define my future. But when times were tough and I looked in the mirror, I was unable to see the potential of what could be. I was locked into what was, along with the shame and regret of choices I made in the past that were bleeding into my present life. I chose then to stop working on myself, allowing the vicious cycle of insecurities, selfishness, and pain I caused to those closest to me to manifest itself. The repetitive behavior of cheating in relationships, lying to those closest to me, and sabotaging myself created a continued path of loneliness and regret for me. Looking back, it cost me so much.

What I didn't realize then was that the leadership journey I had begun was trying to work counter to the choices I was making personally. Over the years, as the emerging leader inside was unknowingly developing, the faults of my past personally bled into the leader I was becoming. I made numerous mistakes in how I led, how I communicated with others, how I treated others, and how I positioned my role in others' lives. I took advantage of my role, instead of being open to learning from it. I took for granted others' willingness to see me as a leader instead of truly understanding the responsibility to others (and myself) that being a leader entails.

Over time and through those failures, I began to realize that I had to make a choice between leading *for* others, or *because of* others. I needed to stop resting on what I thought others expected – and begin to understand what I believed, and begin leading from that place. To learn from my failures and commit myself to becoming the leader that was building inside of me. I began focusing on understanding my mistakes and making new, better choices and steps forward. Ultimately, I began to stop the terrible cycle that was controlling my life.

I began to see how my failures and successes as both a person and a leader were affecting those around me, including those whom I led. I saw how others responded to my leadership and slowly began to connect the dots of my personal and professional life – seeing more clearly how the choices I made on dealing with and learning from the past were impacting both.

Little did I realize then what I know now: By doing so, I was beginning to unleash the leader within – and with it, the much improved, more content, and happier person I am today.

Now, I am committed to a personal journey to understand and change the narrative that has tormented me both personally and professionally. I am realizing that the cheating and lying I was doing to others, along with my actions of taking advantage of people and position, were only cheating and lying to the man in the mirror. In fact, by taking advantage of others, I was sabotaging my own self-growth and limiting the leader that I was aspiring to be.

Now, I am working to live a parallel life of transparency and honesty that can be shared in all aspects of my life. To be truthful in and about my journey reflects the man I am and the leader I strive to be.

I see now that past choices I made often fit social norms or the expectations of others. I remember my mom always pressing for me to lead my brothers and sisters daily. It set an unrealistic expectation of me being their "leader" (through expectation) long past her death in 2016, the result of multiple ailments. I still carry that with me today and have ultimately rejected it by choice and action. My family relationships still are not a strength today, and my actions have not supported that expectation set so many years ago. So this remains a work in progress for me – especially as I focus on living up to my own expectations as opposed to the expectations of others.

On the other hand, I now view my professional life through the lens of meeting others where they are, not just on what is fulfilling me in the moment. After all, if I am not able to fill my own cup, how am I able to fill others' with the transparency and honesty I am asking of them? By sharing my story of emptiness and loneliness through honest words and asking questions of myself while challenging these social norms, I am learning to uncover clarity and ultimately link the past and future "me" to the present. I am wanting to share an understanding of how my life of leadership and the lessons I am learning are intertwined with my past. A past filled with loneliness, bad habits, and repeated mistakes that have plagued me – but also a hard-earned courage to rise above it all.

The latest chapter of my life's story is one of growth, perspective, and honesty. And it is the one of which I am most proud. It can only come from putting in the work of self-assessment and self-reflection. I have looked back now not to blame or make excuses, but to better understand today and give hope for tomorrow.

I am working to shed the narrative of HAVING to be a leader to ACCEPTING the responsibility of being one. That means recognizing that my past is forever a part of me – but it does not fully define me. The path ahead will always be toward progress, but never perfection. I am now able to remain open to the leader I am becoming and the lessons that I have learned along the way.

For so long, the reason I led was for me and what I got out of it. Then I blamed; now I accept. I continue to grow, and I will still fail from time to time. But through the lessons of my past, I am choosing to walk forward into this leader and the person I was born to be.

When I think back to "then," I realize I have lived and made choices for far too long under the umbrella of failure. Now, I know I have come a VERY long way – and it wasn't easy. Then, I viewed myself as a failure. Now, I walk out into the world of possibility and potential as a leader – and more important, as a work in progress.

Come to think of it, isn't that what we all are?

PART II

Lessons in Leadership

CHAPTER 9

Don't Stop Evolving

Coming of age in the 1980s has forever cemented my love of the music of that "totally awesome" decade. In fact, to this day, my favorite song of all time remains Journey's now iconic 1981 megahit, "Don't Stop Believin'." Seriously – who doesn't love that song? Even now, friends will drunk-dial me when someone is performing it during a fun night of bad karaoke, or if the song is being played in the bar, simply because they know all too well how much I absolutely love it.

So I find it both ironic – and profound – that I can't get that song out of my head as I share what I believe to be the first lesson of leadership: Don't Stop Evolving. (I guess in some ways, it could be Don't Stop Believin' as well – but I'll leave it to Steve Perry and the band to speak, or rather sing, to that!)

To evolve means to develop gradually, from a simple to more complex form or to come forth gradually into being.

Isn't that what we do through life?

It's definitely what we do through the leadership journey.

No matter how or when we get started in leadership, we are challenged to evolve with the environment around us or within ourselves. Acknowledging from the onset that we are not perfect and have the need to be open to change goes a long way to set the stage for growth in ourselves and among the teams we lead.

We often hear others say that someone is a "natural leader." But that would be too easy! Maybe there are natural habits or personality traits a "leader" has inside them, but as I self-reflect, my journey as a leader has been far from natural. It has taken lots of work, commitment, openness to learning, and the ability to be self-aware.

One of my biggest leadership lessons came when I realized that earning the title of "manager" did not automatically make me a leader. In fact, all too often, I've witnessed people achieving a promotion to "manager" and suddenly believing that (and behaving like) they are now an entitled leader. My leadership journey and the lessons of my own evolution have taught me differently. First and foremost, I have learned that true leadership is not defined simply by the titles we hold.

Leadership used as a way to hide from others has its limitations. Eventually all we're working to hide becomes exposed and any trust or perceived connection is lost. Why? Because leadership needs to be authentic.

I remember early on in my journey going through a tough time in my life. My grandfather was sick, and inside I was a mess and unable to communicate with my team. I found myself hiding out in my office and feeling the egg shells everyone was either stepping on or trying to avoid. At that time, I was leading from behind – not willing to allow myself to be vulnerable in the moment and share my struggles. The choices I was making were eroding any trust that existed, and my internal weakness was being exposed.

One morning, I got the team together and openly apologized to them. I didn't go into great detail, but I shared generically the challenges I was dealing with, assured them that I saw how I was acting, and that my behavior wasn't how I wanted it to be going forward. This led to an honest, vulnerable moment for all involved, as I gave them opportunities to share how they were feeling about life, work, and our team. When we walked away, I felt more connected, better understood, and personally less isolated. Being authentic was a big step in my evolution as a leader.

I also remember early on making decisions based on how I believed or perceived they would be accepted by my team. Through my insecurities, choices and decisions were made (or more times NOT made) based on the reaction I believed I would get or the rejection I thought I would feel. Looking back, those became some of the worst decisions I made, because they lacked accountability – to others, or selfishly to me. Trusting that a message is heard without accountabilities placed and followed up on is a recipe for lack of productivity.

Another challenging time in my leadership evolution occurred when I was struggling to get buy-in to the sales coaching I was conducting – which I was asked to do by my senior manager. I brought this up to her, and she said something very simple that has remained with me for years now.

"Ethan, even Tiger Woods needs a coach."

This insight came at the peak of Tiger's dominance in the golf world. It spoke so loudly to me, as these seven words encouraged me, motivated me, and gave me the confidence to lead with accountabilities, using Tiger as my "crutch." Those whom I led may not have been Tiger fans, but they knew how good he was at his sport. This is when I began (although slowly) to be a student of leadership and coaching. I started to become increasingly aware of people who were thriving – and realized they weren't doing it exclusively on their own. There was always someone leading them, whether in front, behind, or by their side. Holding them accountable to internal or external goals. I hadn't mastered the techniques, but I was becoming more aware of the influence I had as a leader and coach, and the role I could play in others' lives. In the past, I used my insecurities as a reason to NOT act with accountability or conviction. Today, I am evolving to use my insecurities to lead from strength, not weakness. That strength comes from remaining ever aware of my past. I've learned to gain trust by becoming vulnerable – creating an environment of growth and collaboration, not one of fear and isolation.

Leadership may come easy to some; they may be more natural at it than others. But no matter where you fall on the "leadership spectrum," it will always be a work in progress. To engage with others is work, and to work is to be open to constantly evolving. Sharing this story is work. Sharing the impact it has had on me as a leader is my continuing evolution.

Leadership takes courage. It takes compassion. It takes being able to stand on your own two feet and realize that not all choices or interactions will be liked or well received. But more often than not, if we lead with intent and communicate effectively allowing for feedback and accountability, we create an environment of winning – and the path toward continued evolution becomes clearer.

As the world around us turns, we are constantly asked to evolve and grow with it. No matter the success – or failures – of a leader, remaining open to evolving is critical. The paths to success and self-awareness are not linear. The needs of those around us will always be changing. As leaders, we are tasked with staying open to that change, open to feedback, and open to the signs that present themselves along the way.

Without being open to our own continued evolution, the opportunity for growth, development, and learning subsides. When that happens, leadership ceases and complacency begins, and we lose our ability to accept change.

It's clear that I have learned so much through my failures and successes. As a person and a leader, I am far from perfect and remain committed to evolving on the path in front of me. As I grow in both mindset and actions, the leader inside me grows.

So don't stop evolving!

(And don't stop believing, either.)

CHAPTER 10

Accept Change

If the only constant in life is change, why is it that most of us have such an aversion to it?

Think about it: Not one minute, let alone second, in this life is exactly the same as the other. I believe it isn't the constant nature of change that we don't like, it is the impact that change plays in our world individually that causes the inherent reaction inside us. So the challenge we all face is do we accept change or run from it? I have done both and continue to be challenged in my journey to accept that change is inevitable and intuitively respond accordingly.

Some may look at my story as a tragedy of sorts. I used to and still do harbor resentment at times. But if there is a silver lining to my story, it's that I was exposed to a lot of change and chaos early in life. That forced me to learn how to embrace change amidst day-to-day life. I learned quickly how to adapt to my surroundings. Changing schools? I had to meet new people and make new friends frequently. Moving to a new neighborhood or town? I had to quickly adjust to my new environment. "Adding or subtracting" from the family? Adapt and smile, for that was the expectation handed down to me. Some of the changes were good, others not so much. Sometimes, I chose the wrong way to adapt – or not to adapt at all. That left me treading water while others went swimming by. I let environments around me dictate how I accepted or executed change, as opposed to leading myself through it all proactively.

To choose to accept change takes courage. It often requires choosing the road less traveled, even if the more populated road is more familiar and less bumpy. More times than not, change is the unknown. That unknown path often causes fear. To me, fear is the ultimate motivator. It causes fight or flight.

My leadership journey began with me choosing fear – before ultimately choosing the unknown road and never looking back. Back in 2001, I was in a leadership role at a local financial institution. I was actively recruited to leave that job to lead three offices at a local credit union. In my mind, I didn't deserve the opportunity and I let fear of failure get in the way. To change my life at that time scared me, so I decided to stay put. Fast forward one year, and that same credit union called again. This time, even with the same fear, I ran to it instead of away from it. I took the chance, said yes, and it turned out to be one of the most rewarding times of my career. Yes, life was asking me to change. Yes, I chose fear first out of safety. The second time around, however, I stepped into the change, faced the fear, and was ultimately rewarded with a career path I doubt I would have experienced if I had not made the move.

As leaders we are asked to navigate through that one constant in life – change – all the time. We have the responsibility not only to navigate it for ourselves, but to help those we lead paddle through the unchartered waters, knowing they have fears and uncertainty as well. At times, the environment around us changes so fast. I think back to 2008 and the serious financial crisis that unfolded. At that time, I was an individual producer working as a financial advisor. The changes were happening so quickly around us and we had no control – or at the time, understanding – as to where we or our clients would land and how their lives may be impacted forever. I learned an important leadership lesson from my boss at the time: To care and to communicate. He called me at 7:30 a.m. each day, checked in, reminded me of why I was needed, and showed his unwavering support for me and our team – which was so instrumental. His calls actively demonstrated leadership in a time of drastic change and chaos. His simple actions – the daily phone calls, the checking in, the reassurance – went a long way to propel me through the dark days of that time and became a vivid lesson in leadership that I didn't even realize at the time.

Fast forward twelve years to the COVID pandemic. Now I was the leader. I found myself reaching out to my team daily. Checking in on them, reinforcing their value to themselves and their clients, reminding them that they were not alone. That in the rapidly changing landscape no one understood at the time, that they were cared for and heard. I was there to listen.

One Saturday morning, I sent my former boss a text thanking him for his leadership through the 2008 crisis – letting him know how I leaned on and learned from his example. I wanted to help those I was now leading through their moment of dramatic change.

It is so easy to be paralyzed by change especially if it isn't something we choose – and it rarely is. How we position change to those we lead can be so important when looking for results. Listening to understand before being understood is a great lesson in change management. By taking the time to listen first, we allow courageous steps to be taken by those who are being asked to absorb and change with us.

The opposite of change can be complacency. By not allowing ourselves to fall victim to complacency – whether being comfortable or successful – can go a long way to defining ourselves as leaders. Change in our environment is the core instrument of growth and learning. To be complacent does not allow for our eyes to be open or ourselves to be aware.

ACCEPT CHANGE

Change is a constant, and as leaders we have a responsibility to learn from it and guide others through it. We must show courage in our steps *into* the change instead of finding excuses to step away from it. This includes leading by example, acknowledging fear, and allowing it to motivate brave decision-making that helps us navigate through the ever-changing environment of daily life.

To accept change as a leader and as a person is to accept growth. We grow by developing ourselves in the midst of all the noise that surrounds us, and remaining open to learning from all that comes our way.

As leaders, accepting change is both our challenge and our responsibility.

CHAPTER 11

Lean In and Pour In

I am quite certain that the words "lead" and "lonely" were never intended to be in the same sentence. But they are both the backdrop and forefront of my story.

My journey as a leader has been fueled by the loneliness and emptiness I have carried and continue to carry throughout my life. Over time, however, I am continuing to learn and practice lessons in leadership that have helped fill the void inside. By staying open to others and being intentional in my journey to overcome my internal struggles, I am choosing to *lean into* – and in essence, *pour into* authentically and with purpose – those whom I lead, both personally and professionally.

To me, there is a profound difference between the terms "lean into" and "pour into." And I believe as leaders we have a responsibility to do both.

To lean into another is an action that takes intention. It doesn't always happen naturally. It is an action of trust, an action of self-awareness, and one of connection. To lean in asks the leader to be open, to listen, and to learn. Learn the challenges that are being faced, what excites, what motivates, and most importantly, what is most important in the moment. To lean in doesn't mean you have the answers. It means you are showing that you are a partner in the process of growth. As a leader, you are putting your ego aside to meet at common ground.

Being intentional as a leader is essential in the "leaning in" process. To lean in is to connect and lay the foundation of trust. Nothing more and nothing less. As leaders, we have that responsibility to make it about those we lead and not about us. To me, learning the value of leaning in and putting myself second has gone a long way in helping to begin filling the voids of my past and my feelings of loneliness.

To pour into another is a more proactive act of vulnerability. It's sharing yourself, your coaching, your ideas, and your encouragement. It isn't about opening yourself up completely to the world or who you lead, but to be able to be vulnerable enough to share, guide, and lead based on your experiences, history, and knowledge. To challenge others to become better versions of themselves.

I think a common mistake we make as leaders is to give immediate answers. It is perfectly and wisely OK to take a step back, assess the situation, and create a trusted space for the person receiving our message to absorb it in an environment that is conducive for learning and engagement. To pour into others is not to provide the answers. It is to share thoughts or ideas that will help those we lead find the answers from within and support their journey to get there.

To me as a leader, this was and is one of the hardest lessons to learn. Inherently, it is so easy to be a "fixer." In fact, this has plagued me through my life in relationships, family, or even in my leadership/professional journey. If I hear a problem, I often just jump in and try to fix it. I want to "rescue" people from their apparent challenges or mistakes. In the moment, it felt right and it felt good. Problem solved! Crisis averted!

But what I have learned, however, is that some (or many) of these challenges or problems are not my problems to fix. If I do fix them, how can someone I lead learn? As a leader who now better understands the value of "pouring in," I have discovered that good things happen when the 'fix' or adjustment comes from the person experiencing the challenge at hand. Pouring in…actively listening…and then helping the person understand the situation and find ways to work through it goes a much longer way to his or her personal and professional growth. This is not easy, but it is what great leaders do.

My path toward truly learning the lessons of leadership began by leaning in first. As a former "fixer," I just dove in without emotion or trust, fixed, and moved on. I was reactive in my leadership. I didn't have the awareness to be intentional in action, or the ability to trust others and meet them where they were. Quite honestly, I was selfish. My needs as a leader were met through accolades, pats on the back, and promotions. But I missed the opportunity in front of me by not understanding what it truly meant to lead. It wasn't until I started incorporating one-on-ones into my daily practice and connecting more with my teams both individually and as a group that I started to see that leadership has to be intentional. I was taking it for granted and allowing it to happen to me as opposed to me happening to it and those I led.

Leaning in meant connecting with those who needed me most. For the longest time, I believed they did what their position required, we were doing great, I fixed problems, and life was good. But what I missed and finally learned on the job was that people desire authentic leadership. They need to be cared about. They need to know that their "boss" understands them, their goals, and their desires. And as I began to learn this by leaning in, truly listening, and being available to my team, something good happened to me as well: I was able to fill my own gaps of loneliness and emptiness. I was able to give back to others, create space for greater vulnerability, and trust more in others and myself to pour in as well.

For years, loneliness controlled my life. But I have slowly come to find a silver lining from that terrible sting: Loneliness has served as the catalyst for my leadership journey. And while it still exists, loneliness no longer controls me. Leadership is now the driving force in my life.

Indeed, leadership is my purpose.

With this winner's mindset, I continue to grow through my loneliness and lead from a place of strength – not one of past weakness or fault. Each day, I wake up and strive to be an intentional leader-in-action. One who balances the need to *pour into* others with vulnerability and trust, and *lean into* their experiences with intention and openness.

I can only hope that my hard-earned lessons can help others lean into and pour into wherever they are on their own leadership journey.

CHAPTER 12

Fear Not!

From the day a child is born, that beautiful little baby is looking up at the big world, trying to see clearly what is in front of him or her – trying to understand what comes next. Science would say we are unable to see clearly at that moment.

Although we can't understand fear as a newborn, can you imagine how scared we all must be in those first few minutes in this new world?

From the first moment of our birth, we must rely on others to help teach us ways to see through the haze. We need to learn ways to face fear – and realize that looking up is just our way of launching us toward progress.

As you now know, fear has long been the ultimate motivator to me. But can you imagine as children if inherently we stopped taking our first steps because we were afraid of falling? Or never rode a bike again after the first time we tipped over? It took encouragement from a loved one to get us back up, support us through our fear, and make us try again.

This is true as leaders, too. We are constantly tasked with helping others navigate their "fear of falling" – and fear of failing – and encouraging them to try again.

But how, as leaders, do we help others manage through, and possibly even overcome, their fears?

I believe it begins with intentional actions that are focused squarely on our own self-awareness and willingness to lean into the fear with them – using what I call the "Four C's." I see (or "c"!) these as ways to open the door and ultimately break down fear, confusion, and lack of clarity.

Caring: It has been said that people don't care how much you know until they know how much you care. When taking the role of a leader, we are committed to being in the people business. That said, from the outside looking in, why is caring for people we lead so challenging? I believe it is our responsibility to care about those who are entrusted to us. Caring doesn't need to be intentional; it should be natural. To care about those we lead is the core principle of the Four C's. If you don't care, how do you build trust? How can you authentically connect? Sure, to care comes with boundaries, but if we aren't able to care openly for those we support, what is the foundation we build from and what success can be realized?

Connection: As leaders, we are asked to motivate, inspire, and gain trust. All are critical tasks. But what gets lost at times is the need to be INTENTIONAL in all that we do and how we do it. Leadership is not a switch that we turn on; there are so many levels to it. So at its foundation, a strong leader must connect with their people and remain connected – and I'm not just talking about using technology (although that can certainly be part of it). I'm talking about the intentional act of reaching out, keeping in contact with, and checking in even on the regular day-to-day "stuff." All of this can go a long way to help curb the fear of those we lead. As leaders we need to ask this! If we care enough to connect, do we connect enough to care?

Communication: To communicate seems so simple, but it can often be one of the toughest tasks we have as leaders, especially when it comes to challenging conversations or being vulnerable enough to connect with our people in the first place. Communication is not always easy, but it is essential. Fear in uncertainty can be the worst kind for people and being able to connect and communicate effectively in times of the unknown is important in a leader's journey. And don't forget: Listening is perhaps the most critical (yet often overlooked) part of effective communication. Also, our actions (and body language) almost always speak louder than words.

Consistency: Connecting and communicating are great, but if you are not doing these things consistently, you risk credibility with your teams and risk creating unwarranted fear that can disrupt all good intentions. Communication and connection should be done with discipline and intention. When done consistently, this helps people understand where they stand and where they are going.

Of course, fear is something that leaders face as well: fear of failing, fear of not succeeding, fear of not helping others, and most importantly (and one I felt often) fear of not doing enough or giving my team my all.

As a younger leader, I have failed a lot. I've made bad decisions, connected in the wrong way, led unsuccessful teams, and failed to communicate the goals and accountabilities the proper way. Early on, I ignored those failures and kept making the same mistakes. The fear I was feeling was that of being an impostor. How can I lead people when they are seeing all of my mistakes? I was fearful of losing my job, fearful that those I led would see through me. I became more concerned about "surviving" my failures to mask my fear instead of facing my fears and failures head on and learning from them.

Today, I remain a work in progress. I am a leader who still doesn't get it right all the time. But I continue to learn from my mistakes. I listen more. I challenge more. Most of all, I am more self-aware about not losing myself in my own fears. Instead, I try to understand my fears – and the fears of others – and use them to lead myself and those around me.

I am not perfect, but I don't have to be. And neither do you.

So fear not!

CHAPTER 13

Be Self-Aware, Not Self-Absorbed

"Just don't screw it up."

That's what I thought when, after years of being a financial advisor, I was promoted to a leadership position in 2010. It was one of the most rewarding times in my life – but it required me to lead my peers. I jumped in head first with every intent to continue the trajectory of what my boss had mapped out.

Looking back now and in the excitement of then, it's clear I forgot to look to see if there was water in the pool when I dove in.

I don't believe I screwed it up, but I didn't have a plan. So for all of the successes the team had, I had twice as many failures. Why? In a nutshell, I was not self-aware. I just thought I could show up, treat everyone equally (a big mistake), and the ship would keep moving forward full steam ahead. Looking back, I realize I didn't have the tools for prolonged success. Nor did I have the awareness to find the tools and learn from them.

Sure, I could motivate. I could help drive activities. But navigating a world of leadership with those who once were my peers and friends?! That required something more. But I was more concerned with keeping and holding friendships than being respected and helping to make the team better. I tried to treat each team member equally, but not necessarily fairly. I didn't understand the difference and paid the price in loss of respect and buy-in. I lacked the skills to take a step back and check myself. I made decisions that created a "softer landing" for me than a challenging environment and success for them. What I imagined would be the best time of my career spiraled into one of the most challenging times – simply because I didn't have the awareness to lead myself.

As leaders, we need to know who we are and who we aren't. We also are asked to know the same of the people we are entrusted to lead. To quote inspirational speaker and author Simon Sinek, this isn't a "finite game mentality." To know who we are and aren't is in our evolution as humans and leaders. There may be some traits that form our foundation, but we all remain works in progress. As leaders, being open to that concept can go a long way toward mapping our success. It's important to acknowledge that we can't expect perfection from ourselves.

We can't from others, either.

When we strive to be self-aware, it's nearly impossible to be self-absorbed. We don't just focus on ourselves. We remain aware of the people and the environment around us. This gives perspective in the midst of both the wins we (and others) experience and the challenges we all face.

If an athlete is hurt, we sometimes hear they are "day-to-day" in their recovery. Why is that term used only in recovery? Aren't we all living day-to-day? As leaders, it is our quest and responsibility to remain self-aware and create an environment of growth as we are all working toward progress. Success is infinite. There is life past the goal line, and we are tasked humbly with taking fear of the unknown and creating a path, a strategy for existence and relevance.

The task of being self-aware is not one to take lightly. It requires discipline and intentionality. It is about finding and taking time and carving it out for your growth as a leader through reading, meditation, self assessment, podcasts, and other ways that expand your knowledge and your mindset. Sometimes self-assessment can come from soliciting feedback from trusted members of your team.

Once, I ran a virtual meeting for my team. I walked away truly feeling that I "nailed it" and felt the team walked away clear on expectations and feeling the same way. After the meeting, I reached out to a trusted employee who was on the call and asked for her feedback. She shared the positives, but then shared where she felt I may have missed the mark. Now, was I expecting that? No! I felt I had delivered. But hearing her perspective allowed me to step back, reflect, and see where I could have said or done something more direct and gained more feedback. Her candor helped and gave me the focus and awareness to deliver maybe just a little differently in the future.

Asking for feedback is not always easy, especially as a leader. (That's probably why it doesn't happen as much as it should.) It requires being open to accepting the bad with the good and learning from it. It also requires us to be vulnerable enough to receive and act if necessary.

The key to self-awareness is to be intentional and disciplined, and then taking the time to reflect and be open to pivoting as needed. Yes, being self-aware can leave us vulnerable to fear and failure. But if we realize that through learning we become stronger, not weaker, we are positioning ourselves and our teams for a healthier, more collaborative path toward success.

CHAPTER 14

Learn from Mistakes and Failure

Failing is not fun.

In fact, failure is such a hard word to absorb.

To fail at something – anything – is met with disappointment, anger, frustration, and self-doubt. None of these feelings bring about a very positive emotion.

The fear of failing and of making mistakes is embedded in us early in life. As leaders, we are challenged not only to navigate through our own failures of the present and past, but also to help others steer through theirs.

In 2003, I was changing jobs and roles from a manager to a financial advisor. To do that, I needed to pass several exams that would allow me to offer products and services to potential clients. I never was a great test-taker and I struggled both conceptually and tactically with the exams.

I failed multiple times. Each time I failed, there was a part of me that questioned my path. Self-doubt crept in. Sure, I had the support of my boss, the people I worked with, and even my family, but I questioned myself and my abilities and almost quit the goal before I even got started. Looking back, my life would look so different now if I had packed it in and walked away from the opportunity.

But what I have come to realize was that it was OK to lean on and trust the support of others. To take the time I needed to ultimately get through the exams and understand that there were others like me. I didn't have to be perfect; I did have to commit to trying my best and studying hard. Ultimately, I passed the tests.

Looking back, choosing to stand up to failure began to change how I viewed it.

Early on in life – whether in stories I shared or choices I made in early relationships, jobs, and opportunities – I always chose the less risky path to avoid the potential of failing. In 2003, it would have been easy to just walk away from that new opportunity, keep doing what I was doing, and take the easy path. But I chose to stand up to the failure I was experiencing and use it as an opportunity to learn. Since then, I have coached many financial advisors through the exam process. There have been failures, but I am able to use my story as an example of fortitude and what awaits on the other side.

Learn from Mistakes and Failure

Self-worth is affirmed and enhanced through failure and learning from it. We are all going to make mistakes and fail from time to time. It is how we respond to that failure that defines the next steps and opportunities that await.

As children, failing often would lead to "punishment" of some kind. To fail a test resulted in a bad grade. To fail riding a bike resulted in scrapes on your knees. To fail at telling the truth led to trouble at home. In my house, there was always an emphasis on consequences, never a focus on what could be learned or what lesson could be gained. As I grew up, failure led to embarrassment in the moment, emotional hurt, physical pain, and confusion. So failure led me to ignore and to avoid. Unfortunately, I personalized my failures and chose to not learn from them. All this taught me early on was to make safe choices – because making a mistake or failing led me to be punished somehow.

I am not saying that making mistakes and failing shouldn't have consequences. But as leaders, we should work to create environments in which failing is OK if trying your best, allowing for growth and affirming that no one is expected to be perfect.

Failure associated with fear on all levels triggers strong reactions in people. Most run away, but some learn to face the situation, overcome it, and grow from it. As leaders, we are challenged to take the fear of failure and encourage those around us to lean in and learn from it. After all, haven't we all made mistakes in our lives? Whether we realize it or not, those mistakes and our reactions to them have helped shape us.

Leaders must work to teach through the mistakes and empower those around us. This requires us to be comfortable being uncomfortable. To be vulnerable enough to share our mistakes with those we lead. And to share what we learned and how failing helped to mold the leader and person we are today.

In the moment, failure of any kind doesn't feel good. It can even cripple us if we aren't open enough to accept that we aren't perfect. I look back on my life and see that for so long, I was unable to learn from my failures and mistakes. I blamed others. After I blamed them, I defended my actions because of failures I had made in the past. It wasn't until I started accepting that I wasn't perfect, acknowledging I was going to fail and make mistakes from time to time, and trying to learn from them that I became a more self-aware person and a more vulnerable and open leader. This allowed me to build stronger connections with my team, create environments of trust, and grow as a person and leader.

All these years later, I still look back with shame and regret at my failures of the past. However, I now accept them as part of who I am and as part of my why. They are a reason, not an excuse.

Learn from Mistakes and Failure

As a leader, I challenge myself everyday to ensure that the people I lead look at themselves through the lens of opportunity, not regret. I strive to inspire them to work toward progress, not perfection. And to trust those in their circle to help pick them up when they make a mistake or fail. Because they will – and you will. But by learning from it, we become better people and leaders.

Here's the truth: We are born to make mistakes, and at times we will fail. But we are also born to learn.

It all begins and ends there!

CHAPTER 15

Listen...
and Gain Perspective

Do you know that the words LISTEN and SILENT have the exact same letters? We all know the English language is quirky, but how ironic – and how perfect.

As leaders, this is great food for thought as we dive into the topic of listening.

To listen seems so easy, but is it, really? We HEAR a lot of things, but are we actively listening? And are we silent long enough to even begin to think about what we've heard?

To listen is to gain an understanding of the person or people with whom you are communicating. When we actively listen, we open ourselves up to the perspectives of others and create a path of open dialogue and continued learning.

Simply said, to listen is to gain perspective.

As leaders, we are not selling anything. Listening is about connecting with our people and our teams. It's ensuring they feel heard and remaining open to learning WITH them. But the truth is, most of us are better at speaking than we are at listening. Listening allows for conversation "with" as opposed to talking "to." And the silence that genuine listening brings about really is, as they say, golden.

The word *perspective* plays such a critical role in leadership. As leaders, we need to be open to the perspectives of others. Without doing so, our perspective stops. We also have perspective to share – and should do so at the proper time. So the challenge is to create an environment that allows for open discussion.

One way to do this is in meetings, either in a group setting or one-on-one. Are you creating opportunities to talk WITH your team or are you talking TO them? The more we listen, the more we gain an understanding of those we are working with, which allows us to meet them where they are.

I believe that leaders become more effective the more they allow for others' ideas to be shared and discussed. This starts with listening and creating an environment of trust through an honest exchange of words and ideas. This may not always be easy, but the goal is to be open, to not judge, and to encourage others to do the same.

This does not come without the need to take time for yourself so you are able to take time to help others you serve. It's about the Three L's: listen, learn and then lead.

Listening takes discipline. It requires us to be present in the moment, to be open enough to ask for understanding when needed, and to ask clarifying questions if needed. Listening allows us to discover the emotion of what is being discussed. To hear perspective – and even if you don't agree, being open to learn from it. When we listen to another person's perspective, it may change ours or theirs – and that is where change of behavior happens.

If we are listening effectively, we can learn more easily. Our ability to stay open to others' perspectives will only enhance the conversation and our leadership journey. Remember this: When you change the way you look at things, the things you look at change. Listening to and learning from others changes perspectives and allows us to grow.

And when we do this, we are able to lead more effectively and with greater clarity.

As leaders, we must, as always, remain self-aware – allowing ourselves some time and space to listen to different perspectives, learn from them, and have the energy to lead from what we have learned. That learning helps with HOW we lead each person with whom we work.

I think back to changes that happened in my organizations at times. Early on, I was a leader who was one-sided.

I shared my thoughts and perspectives and what I felt was needed to make the necessary changes to get the task accomplished, whatever it may have been. I ignored the engagement needed. I ignored sharing the why. And I focused on the "what" and just expected change to happen. Because of this, change was slow or non-existent. Targets were not met, and I was left to feel like I had to do it all. When looking back, my team was capable – they just didn't understand my perspective being thrown AT them, and I didn't create the environment for them to share their thoughts and perspective at any point in the process.

The result was resentment and lack of trust.

Looking back, and through my increasing self-awareness, I have seen growth throughout my career as a listener and a leader. When I started as a manager at a new company a few years ago, I had a meeting with a clearly disgruntled and frustrated employee. I'll call him Joe.

Joe shared with me all that had been thrown at him and that he didn't feel like he had a voice. Our initial conversation was two hours. I listened, and I shared perspective from my limited view. We had additional calls and meetings, but each was productive. I was self-aware enough to ensure that our conversations were never about me. They were always about Joe, listening to his perspective, and creating a new plan for him that ended up creating a positive path – ultimately leading to his two best years ever.

Did his job change? No.

Did his tasks change? No.

What did change? Joe's perspective, my perspective, and the level of communication and listening – all leading to greater trust and transparency. All of it wasn't necessarily what he wanted to hear. But in the end, he better understood the field he played on, and ultimately, how he could play the game going forward.

Listening and gaining perspective go hand in hand. It isn't always easy, and it must be intentional. It takes discipline and focus. But there's no denying it: Our commitment to active listening and helping others understand the value of their perspective simply makes us better leaders.

So listen up!

CHAPTER 16

Remove The Masks: Forgive, Accept, and Be Vulnerable

As human beings, we all have moments when we find our self-worth challenged.

Mine was ripped away early in life, and I didn't have the tools to rebuild or even potentially develop it. For decades, I thought and believed that I had no value, no self-worth at all. My ability to love and accept love continues to be challenged today. The confidence I have in myself is still far outweighed by the confidence I invest in and try to bring forth in others.

We all have masks, which we wear from time to time – especially in the workplace. My masks have taken on many shapes and sizes throughout my life. No matter which mask

I wore, the common goal was to hide my fear of my own worth.

Did all of that start with my emptiness? My loneliness? The abuse I endured? With not being able to fill the void?

To me, self-worth comes with forgiving and accepting one's self. This difficult act, just like my journey as a leader, is a work in progress.

To accept myself, my failures, my hurt, and the pain I feel and have caused myself and others is asking me to forgive myself. To forgive my actions and my mistakes. It begins with asking myself to first accept them. Honestly, I am not fully ready yet. I am still evolving.

ABoyet as I work to forgive and accept, I have come to learn and believe that I do have self-worth.

As I have been able to find value in myself, I also am able to allow more people in and let go of my fears, doubts, and the fear of being seen.

To lead others, we must lead ourselves first. This doesn't happen in a straight line at all. As leaders, the path to connecting with those we lead begins with the relationship we have with ourselves. By acknowledging and accepting that I am a work in progress, I feel a strength that allows me to have realistic expectations of those I work with and meet them where they are on their own journey. If I am battling internal struggles, it's likely that others are, too. To recognize self-doubt in others and support them by communicating, listening, and challenging them to see beyond the moment is a responsibility that we leaders have.

I've spoken to my journey of leadership and I truly feel this is where I feel most "normal." I am a relational leader – often wearing a mask that allows me to share just enough so that no one NEEDS to pull the mask off. I am able to pour into and lean into people without exposing my truths. When others succeed or thrive, my void is filled at the moment and my self-worth is validated. This book is the beginning of me pulling the mask fully off – to connect authentically as me. Validated in my work, but vulnerable in risk.

The path to forgive and accept is real for me, as is learning to piece back together or just build my own sense of self-worth.

As leaders, we can help others find their worth in their pursuit of growth and success. But it isn't linear. People have their own unique path to follow; as a leader, we have the opportunity to personalize their experiences and support them and their needs. By listening and reflecting, we can find what defines success for them and support the execution of it. This may not always be black and white. Life has a way of throwing gray into it. When that happens, leaders are asked to help find the clarity – since the gray can sometimes be when self-doubt creeps in.

I was once having a coaching session with one of my advisors, and he openly shared that he was in a place of self-doubt. He was trying to understand his place in the organization and was questioning his value. I listened to him and asked questions to see why he felt this way. We then talked about "impostor syndrome."

Impostor syndrome, by definition, is the persistent inability to believe that your success is deserved or has been legitimately achieved as a result of your own efforts or skills.

Whoa, stop! Can I relate to this?

YES!

I was introduced to this concept a few years ago when I started writing this book. I was living the definition, but never knew it was "a thing."

When the advisor and I discussed impostor syndrome, he opened up about his fears, and his feeling of not being good enough. It was a raw, open conversation that opened my eyes as the leader as to what support he needed – and helped open his eyes as well. Since that conversation – and the plan we outlined to move forward – the individual's conviction and confidence are as different as night and day. Will he slip back at times? Absolutely – I am fully expecting it. But when that time comes, we are connected enough now that we will be able to look back, accept what may or may not have happened to make him feel that way, and move forward.

I truly doubt that I could have had that discussion if I hadn't been open to my own journey of self-acceptance and forgiveness. I am not saying we all have to have those moments internally to connect so deeply with those we lead. But being aware of experiences similar to those we lead and being vulnerable enough to "go there" speaks to the influence we can have as leaders.

Leadership is all encompassing. It is about them and us. Without the foundation of who we are as leaders and the willingness to forgive and learn ourselves, our abilities always will be clouded in self-doubt, impostor syndrome, and by the masks that we wear.

As leaders, the journey of developing self-worth should be as infinite as the guidance we provide those we lead. Using our own journey to create vulnerable discussions and connections helps us facilitate growth.

So it's time to remove the masks that often hold us back! It's not always easy. In fact, to look back, forgive ourselves, accept where we are at this very moment, and be vulnerable takes courage, strength, and intentionality.

But focusing on YOU will only help enhance your focus on THEM. And that's what great leadership is all about.

CHAPTER 17

Be Courageous

The remarkable Nelson Mandela once said, "I learned that courage was not the absence of fear, but the triumph over it. The brave man is not he who does not feel afraid, but he who conquers that fear."

Much of what I have opened up about in my life's journey and the leadership lessons I have shared speak to being aware of opportunities to learn. Remaining open to learning can be scary at times and often takes great courage. Learning new things and opening ourselves up can force self-realizations that are sometimes hard to swallow, but can also enhance the strengths we have or want to develop.

As we all know, there is no simple manual on how to become a great leader. We all bring different strengths to the table and different pasts that mold our perspectives. Throughout my career, I have been part of organizations that have taken a "cookie-cutter" approach to leadership

– implying that people in management are "automatically" leaders. More often than not, there is a difference! One of the approaches is reactive and scripted. The other – the intentional approach of leadership – is not reactive. Instead, it is the courageous act of individuals putting themselves out there to connect and bring out the most out in those whom they lead.

I do believe we lead by learning – not in spite of it. We just need to be courageous enough to admit we don't know it all.

Former President Theodore Roosevelt coined a well-traveled phrase: "People don't care how much you know until they know how much you care." As leaders, we have a responsibility to show empathy, to listen, and most importantly to actively communicate with those who look to us. To be a leader, we must have an understanding of self – or the journey will force us there.

Longevity of leadership is built on the desire for people and their success, knowing it never ends. There will always be goals, but the inherent nature to succeed becomes a part of you. It doesn't happen because of you. The challenge becomes infinite. Leadership is not "done" when a goal is achieved. In fact, that's where the courage starts and the real work begins: to learn why you won, to not become complacent, and realize that crossing the goal line wasn't easy. Winning is the catalyst to learn more, to dig in, and to stay open to perspectives so the winning continues and the people involved stay engaged.

We lead by preparation, not by happenstance. John Wooden, perhaps the greatest college basketball coach of all time, once said, "When opportunity comes, it is too late to prepare." So as leaders, we must learn each day to prepare for the next by doing the best that is in front of us at that moment. The goal is to be better today than we were yesterday, so we can be better tomorrow than we were today.

Preparation can mean many different things to people. Think about a simple meeting. As a leader, I used to just bring people together for a meeting and hope for the best, whether I was meeting individually or with a group. By winging it, communication and engagement were pretty much non-existent. It was just me talking. When I asked for feedback, of course there was none. I was left feeling defeated whenever a meeting was done.

I finally realized it: if I'm not prepared, how can I expect my people to be?

So I began preparing a simple agenda in advance of my meetings – outlining the topics to talk about and sharing it in advance. None of this was rocket science, of course, but this simple task proved to be a powerful way to create a whole new vibe with my team. Discussion became more productive, engagement increased, and the team seemed more empowered since I encouraged them to share individually.

All too often, we can get stuck in the cycle of blaming the past for everything that's wrong today. (That used to be me.) It takes courage to learn from the past and be bold enough to make changes when necessary. That's how we avoid making the same mistakes we once did.

As leaders, we can use the past as a foundation for preparation, always learning so we can impact others around us and help them to succeed. And it's not just learning from our past; we must remain open to learning from others. Who is your circle? Do you have that circle of trust? And beyond that circle, are you open to learning from those you lead? All of this takes a form of courage and trust. To learn begins with sharing. For the longest time, this was always a struggle for me – and at times still is. So I ask myself: what can others learn from me? What can I share that will make an impact on others?

Learning to lead is learning courage, learning to be humble, and learning to create an environment of trust. It can't be done in a day. It takes time, intentionality, desire, and discipline. It can't be faked or masked. As long as we lead, we will always be learning – and we will always need to be courageous in that journey.

There is a saying that life is about the pursuit of happiness. I challenge that. Life can't be about the pursuit of anything until you have the courage to pursue. I think of courage as a presence of something inside of you that needs to be unlocked and unleashed.

I lost my courage early on in my life because of my feelings of deep loneliness. Sometimes, I challenge myself that I never had the courage I wanted or needed. I have lived more of my life with a fear of failure, and that I often have felt alone. Instead of facing my fears or trying to develop courage, I surrounded and masked myself in what turned out to be superficial friendships or relationships. I was all about "the quick fix." My focus was always on the perception of perfection. I kept failing because I couldn't find the courage it takes to live intentionally.

Through the lessons of leadership, I have learned to be courageous enough to acknowledge my imperfections. I own my mistakes. There is a lot of my story still to be written and a lot of work still to be done. I will still make mistakes. And I still have fears. But here's where I stand today: I am committed to continuing to pour into those in my circle and beyond, and openly receive and learn much from them. As my journey continues, my focus is on courageously accepting pain, continuing to forgive myself, and in that work finding the self-worth that will only help to fill my emptiness.

This is my story. But I am sure that there are similar stories out there. My experiences can't be changed, but I no longer see myself as a victim. Through the courage and conviction I continue to pursue, I hope to inspire and strengthen my own children's lives. And through my journey of leadership over loneliness, I hope to help others find their courage and enhance their strengths to move beyond their past mistakes.

This is about me standing up and wanting to stop cycles. To remind others that there is a choice. To show that at any stage in life, there is always work to be done. You don't have to let your past control your present.

It's not easy to be courageous. But when you find your courage and use it well, the past no longer has to control your present.

My fight to acceptance is underway. So is my transformation!

CHAPTER 18

Mindset Matters!

As my evolution as a leader has grown, my focus on the importance of mindset has grown as well.

I'm guessing you won't *mind* if I explain?

Simply put, our mindset is our personal set of beliefs that shape how we make sense of the world and ourselves.

When I reflect on my own story, I can now see that my mindset throughout most of my life was reactive and one of blame. I didn't have the discipline to look inside or lead myself. I reacted and made decisions in the moment and without recourse. I didn't realize that by not putting in the work – focusing on myself and my mindset – I was damaging my brand, my credibility as a leader, and most importantly, myself. I was unable and unwilling to look in the mirror first. So I was quick to unleash my "untamed" leadership on those who had no choice but to try and figure me out.

Good luck with that!

Then I saw a television interview with NFL Hall of Fame coach, Bill Parcells, who talked about sharing a poem with his team written by Peter Dale Wimbrow in 1934. It's about "the man in the glass" – and it froze me in my tracks. The message of the poem is that we are ultimately accountable to ourselves. If we cheat ourselves, we cheat others and vice versa. It ends with these powerful words:

"...you can fool the whole world down the pathway of years
And get pats on the back as you pass
But the final reward will be heartache and tears
If you've cheated the man in the glass."

The words really struck me – and have stuck with me for many years now. When I first heard them, they stung. I remember feeling like I had been punched in the gut. I understood the words, but at that moment I felt like they were talking directly to ME! I realized how much of a disservice I was doing by cheating myself. At that time, I didn't understand intentionality. I didn't understand awareness. And I definitely didn't understand discipline and accountability to myself.

Believe it or not, that's how my mindset journey began. It was not intentional at first, but as those words gnawed at me, I consciously began looking at myself in the mirror more and more… and began making decisions with more intention and less reaction when it came to leadership and my day-to-day growth.

As I have made my way along the "mindset journey," I have come to realize that a growth mindset is all about the Three A's: awareness, attitude, and adaptability.

Awareness: For me, it all and ends begins with awareness of self. In fact, my transformation as both a person and a leader is strong testimony to the importance of becoming self-aware. That said, the strengths that emerge from self-awareness are among the hardest lessons to learn, and are still a work in progress for me.

Leaders are asked to motivate, to inspire, and to gain trust. All are critical tasks. But what gets lost at times is the need to be disciplined in all that we do and how we do it. Leadership is not a switch that we turn on and off. There are so many levels to it. But at its foundation, to be a leader is to be connected. We are unable to truly connect with others if we are unable to connect with ourselves. Moreover, leaders are being watched by the people they lead. They are looking at our actions, listening for our words, and responding to how we react to changes or situations that may arise. Our ability to be aware in the moment, to prepare before the moment, and to reflect after the moment go a long way in our growth and in developing credibility with our teams and their own growth mindset.

Attitude: I used to believe that attitude was everything. Show up and "bring the thunder" so to speak and all will follow suit. Others will then take the lightning and run with it – and life will be good. But I have learned over time that all the pomp and circumstance in the world cannot inspire without substance behind it. You can't "fake it 'til you make it" as a leader. It may work for a time, but transparency eventually wins.

John Maxwell says that "attitude isn't everything." It is important – don't get me wrong. As a leader with a growth mindset, you can't show up being "Eeyore" every day. Attitude is the difference maker. But it has to be supported with competence, empathy, and with the realization that it can't change the facts that surround you or your team.

I am intentional with my attitude in every situation. I can control it. I may not be able to control five minutes from now, but my attitude as a leader remains a focus for me always. Attitudes change depending on the situation, so it is on us to control how our attitude shows and what others experience.

Maya Angelou wisely said, "If you don't like something, change it. If you can't change it, change your attitude. Don't complain."

That's some great advice to follow.

Adaptability: The final "A" to remember about mindset is adaptability – the need to be aware enough to pivot when the environment changes around you, accept the change, and move with it, not against it. Leaders are forced to accept change on a daily or sometimes hourly basis, and most times we simply can't control it. How flexible we are, how aware we are, and ultimately, the attitude we have to navigate through the directional shifts that happen can quickly define success or failure.

My good friend Derek Avera from Focus 3 — a boutique consulting firm specializing in leadership, culture, and performance — speaks about the "R Factor."

He uses the equation E+R=O.

Here's what he means: There are always events (E) that happen in our lives. How we respond (R) will in turn help define the outcome (O). If we are reactive in our response, the outcome we are hoping for may not lead to the best result. Instead, adapting and pivoting in times of change and challenge require awareness and attitude to help create engagement and the right mindset for all involved.

Having a growth mindset opens us up to all possibilities, with no end in sight. There is no end game, no goal line. There is just greater opportunity to get better. It is like the overtime rules in college football or extra innings in baseball: There is no clock that counts down; each team keeps strategizing and goes back and forth until there is a winner. Then you know what happens? You get right back at it tomorrow. You learn from the win or the challenge, adjust your attitude, and make the necessary adjustments for the next time. And that's exactly what a growth mindset is all about.

To put it succinctly, mindset truly matters. This is an invaluable lesson to learn – in life and leadership, which is exactly why I chose to close this section of my book with it. It's not only important to have a growth mindset, I believe it's critical to always be chasing one. Doing so sets the tone that we won't stand still. Instead, we are forever looking to grow – and when we grow, others around us will do so as well.

Thanks to a growth mindset – and the other lessons in leadership I have developed slowly over time and have shared within these pages – the man in the glass now smiles back at me. He no longer feels cheated. Or not worthy. Or overwhelmed by loneliness. He still feels vulnerable at times, and that's OK. But he also feels valued and validated – and even victorious at times – on his continuing journey as both a man and a leader.

Thank you, leadership, for unleashing that man in the glass from his life of loneliness and leading him to a more accepting, fulfilling, and rewarding way of life.

I recognize that man in the glass so much more these days.

He's a good guy…a believer…a survivor…and a leader who will always be a work in progress.

And he has no doubt that leadership can do great things for you, just like it has for him.

UNLEASHED

The Leader and the Man Within

As I wrap this final chapter of my book and another chapter of my own story, I remind myself of one thing: Life is unscripted. There are signs everywhere if you are open to seeing them. My story has taken many twists and turns, some of which I understand, and some that have opened up to me by writing and sharing this book.

In a twist of fate that I never could have imagined, these pages began with me sharing the incredible impact and inspiration of my father-in-law – and how his death became the catalyst to so much growth and change inside of me. Today, as I write these closing pages, I find myself spending quality time with my now 80-year-old father, who has been battling cancer and recently entered hospice. He is in his final weeks or months of life.

Life.

We can't control it. But we certainly must cherish it.

That's what I always try to remember — in good times and bad. Sadly, just days after I received the initial manuscript for this book, my father passed away. As I reflect on the deep meaning of all of this, I find the symmetry and parallel nature of this difficult moment – and the journey of these two men who influenced my life in some powerful and complicated ways – much more than ironic. It is poetic and profound.

Looking back, I used to let life and the moments inside own me. What I have come to learn through this leadership journey is that it is OK for me to stand up and own those same moments. To stop looking back and blaming, take them for the lessons they have taught, and accept that it is OK not being perfect.

I have been given this opportunity to share my story and the many lessons I have learned. There is no magic wand that appears and makes the path ahead clear. The lessons of discipline, awareness, and intentionality are ones that I need to carry with me each and every day. I must remember to lead others with a servant mentality. But what about myself? I must lead first and with deliberate action and intent. I may not know the path ahead, but I need to understand the moment, be open to adapting, and never forget that I am always evolving.

Evolution is gradual. In our society of "immediate and now," the path of self-evolution and the growth and evolution of others speaks an entirely different language. It preaches patience, embraces the ability to shut out the noise, and reminds us that Rome wasn't built in a day.

These are such critical lessons in leadership – and in life.

The world needs good leaders. People who value others above themselves, and possess a willingness to look inside, not blame, and be OK with what has happened. We are all works in progress. I hope that through caring about others and communicating consistently as leaders we are able to connect more with those around us and build clarity as we face the unknown ahead of us.

I wrote this book to share my journey, my challenges, my wins, and my lessons learned – and to help inspire others. So I thought I'd close with a letter I've written to my younger self – words of wisdom that would have inspired me at age 5, 10, 20, 30, or beyond. I'd like to pay it forward, and can only hope that this book and/or letter can help, in some small way, unleash the leader within you.

Dear E,

It's funny to think that one of the reasons you were given the name Ethan was because there wasn't a nickname for it. But thinking back, E was and is still what you are called by so many to this day.

I am writing to let you know that all is OK. So much is happening around you that you understand as "normal." Maybe it is and maybe it isn't, but it is the normal you know. Your normal comes with pain, confusion, and lots of chaos. Your normal is intertwined with questions left unanswered, steps not taken, and an emptiness you can't define.

What I want to share with you today is to remember that little boy at the YMCA trying to decide if he was going to jump into the deep end. And the young boy who was going to step on stage in front of a crowd to sing and act in musicals. That boy is now a competent and confident man who has written a book and started his own business.

Be THAT person! Jump. Be locked into your dreams. Be all in with everything you do. Choose the uncomfortable, but learn what safety and comfort are. Being content is OK, and you will find happiness inside of it.

Understand that pain happens. That everyone's past experiences limit or accelerate what they can offer you. Stay aware not just of your surroundings, but of yourself. Be confident in your choices, and know that you will fail and that, too, is OK. Don't fear it, embrace it. Lead from the front. Don't chase people or things. Chase your drive to succeed. Chase your desire to help others. And lastly, chase your journey and what lies ahead without fear.

E, you are going to be OK. Life and growth are not linear. There will always be obstacles in your way, but you are meant to lead others. Just don't forget to lead yourself around and through the barriers as they arrive.

Rise up! Unleash the leader within. Become who you are authentically meant to be. And know it will always be OK to jump in that pool.

I am so proud of you.

Love,
E

Acknowledgements

There I am — 5 or 6 years old at the local YMCA. I had a styrofoam bubble attached to my back. I remember there was an instructor treading water in the deep end of the pool imploring me to jump. Seeing this big, Olympic-size pool that I had been in so many times before seemed scary and caused me much hesitation. It was the same water, same instructor, same smells, same environment. But what was different? It was the unknown of what was going to happen when I jumped in. The safety of the shallow end and what I knew were shifting. I was being asked to jump into a body of water where I didn't see any footing or a bottom. Just a woman and a bubble on my back.

What happened?

I jumped!

Fast forward to today. I am now in my early fifties. I had been collecting stories and ideas, "wanting to write my story" – to share my journey of imperfection to where I am today. To share my lessons learned to hopefully help others.

But as I reflect, I see that in many ways I have been that young boy 45 years ago at the edge of the pool – trying to shed the comfort of the shallow end and jump into the deep end. This book, my story, and whatever transpires from here is me jumping into the deep end – being all in.

There are so many people who I want to thank and honor. First and foremost is my immediate family: Megan, Landon, and Emma. They have experienced a lot behind the scenes. They have seen me fall, fail, and get back up. They have always been there to help guide me – to see what is as opposed to what isn't or what I thought wasn't. Their love, support, and acceptance of me amidst it all was evident in my work on my story and this book.

I dedicate this book to my mom and dad. After reading this, you're likely surprised by this. But I feel they did the best they could with the skill sets they had. They made choices like we all do – some good, some not-so-good. But without them being married and having a son, this story could never be told and I wouldn't be here to share and tell it.

I want to thank the numerous leaders that I have crossed paths with at different times in my life. Four prominent ones played key roles in my development: Vic, Dan, Leo, and Paul. You know who you are! I am forever grateful for the impact you had and still have on me, and the lessons you taught me in actions or in words.

ACKNOWLEDGEMENTS

I also want to thank my "head writing and editing coach" on this journey, Martial. You are my accountability partner. You took my words and helped me create a vision, and now it's a BOOK! I have been "martialized" and am so much better for it. Thank you!

Finally, this book is written for those who read it. I firmly believe everyone has a story to tell. I am not unique in this way. I just hope that my story and what I have learned can help anyone searching for the leader within – and that this book can help you boldly jump into the deep end.

We know that perfection doesn't exist; it is about the daily work, the grind, and the awareness that we are all a work in progress. It's also about realizing that where you have been is not where you necessarily have to be now.

Thank you for reading my book. Here's to investing in yourself and embracing exciting new chapters that lie ahead!